Taming A Shark

How to Build The Confidence and Self Esteem To Do The Things That Scare You The Most

Benjamin A. Portnoy

Copyright © 2014 by Benjamin A Portnoy & Courage, Inc.
All rights reserved.

FIRST EDITION.
ISBN-13: 978-0692283844 (Courage, Inc.)
ISBN-10: 0692283846

Acknowledgements

I mention many of my teachers by name throughout this book.

However, I wouldn't have the same drive, confidence, wisdom, and success if it weren't for the following people. You have all inspired me in more ways than I can count.

***To Mom and Dad**, who have been the GPS to find my life's destinations, even when we disagreed on the route.*
***To Ubby**, who's defined himself by constantly challenging boundaries, whether they came from Marvin or mountains.*
***To Lauren**, whose pursuit of passions helped shape and light my own fires.*
***To Annie**, who knows what she wants and isn't afraid to beat down doors to get it.*
***To Dave**, who has led a life of style, service, grace, and humility in the face of pain so great that I can't even begin to fathom.*
***To my wife Katrina**, who has helped me not only discover, but conquer parts of life I had no idea I was afraid of. You're my beautiful, wonderful partner and you make the scary things much less so.*

I love you.

About The Author

Benjamin A. Portnoy is an author, speaker, trainer, and coach whose focus is helping individuals to overcome fears and anxieties. He has a degree in Journalism from the University of Missouri – Columbia.

He has logged thousands of hours on stages across the country as both a speaker and performer, in front of up to 3,000 audience members at a time.

He lives with his beautiful wife Katrina and their two cats in sunny Austin, Texas, where spend their free time experimenting with wine and vegetarian cooking.

And as of December 2014, he will have conquered his biggest fear...diving with sharks on the North Shore of Oahu in Hawaii.

INSIDE...

Chapter 1: How to Tame a Shark

Chapter 2: Meaning and Purpose

Chapter 3: Our Perception of Risk

Chapter 4: Negative Reinforcement: *It's Not You. It's Me.*

Chapter 5: Our Vulnerabilities to Fear

Chapter 6: Action + Motivation

Chapter 7: The Most Important Skill You Can Learn

Chapter 8: The Anti-Anxiety Toolbox

Chapter 9: Conclusion and Bonus

Chapter 1:
How to Tame a Shark

I was afraid to sit down on the toilet for a week.

Sharks are probably the most feared creature on the planet. They strike terror and dread into virtually every living thing they encounter. Swimming at the top of the food chain, they're pretty much the scariest thing out there.

I learned this lesson well when I was a mere seven years old. It was a quiet weekend at home, and my mom was out shopping. My dad asked if I wanted to watch a movie called *Jaws*.

130 minutes later, my dad had to hastily scoop me up from my fetal position behind the couch.

Even in seven years, I had come across many animals. I had grown up with a dog, petted a cat or two at friends' houses, and even seen bears and alligators through steel bars at the Zoo. But before that day, I had *never* been aware of such a demonic, malevolent, unbeatable creature as the Great White Shark.

That one movie instilled such a drastic fear in me that I was afraid to sit down on the toilet for a week. I mean, Jaws made his way through the water, and my pre-adolescent logic dictated, of course, that it meant he could navigate his way through the St. Louis Municipal Sewer, defy gravity, and squeeze that 25-foot shark body through that tiny toilet hole to swallow me in a single chomp.

However...with that fear, arrived equal levels of amazement.

I mean, here was an animal that could chew a hole in the side of a boat and swallow sailors whole. But in the end, Chief Brody was able to blow it into smithereens. Twice.

Amazing.

And for a seven-year old with a future of crippling anxiety and panic attacks only a few years in front of him, this was incredible. It showed me that, even in the face of the scariest f*cking thing on the planet, there was a way to beat the odds and surmount the insurmountable.

So began my equal fear and fascination of Great White Sharks, and all other sharks for that matter. I was (not literally) consumed by them and wanted to learn all I could. Since then, I've spent hundreds of hours researching sharks; watching, reading, and studying anything I could get my hands on that involved these toothy enigmas.

It was in this pursuit I learned about "tonic immobility."

This is a biological phenomenon where another creature (typically one possessing thumbs) places its hands on the sides of of the shark's snout, and for up to about fifteen minutes, the shark actually enters a near-catatonic state. It becomes hypnotized and virtually paralyzed, to the point where you can do whatever you want with it; pet it, kiss it, take selfies with it, and it is under your (relative) control.

Don't believe it? Google "shark tonic immobility" and watch the videos.

Placing a shark into a tonic state doesn't work the same way each time – you'll see plenty of instances where it doesn't work. But after trial and error and quite a bit of practice, a diver gets a shark to go tonic. And although I've not yet had this experience, I would imagine that anyone who makes it happen is never the same.

I mean, think about it. If you could take the source of the world's greatest dread *literally* into your hands and turn it into putty in your hands, what would that do to your fears? To be able to set aside every nerve, internal warning alarm, and self-defense mechanism, and turn the scariest thing in the world into a purring, little kitten...how would that feel?

It's with that I offer you *Taming a Shark*. What follows is a collection of stories, studies, and exercises based on not only my experience, but the extensive research and and lessons of some of my most admired teachers. I've designed this book to help you get over any fear that has been holding you back from achieving your biggest goals and dreams, and be able to stare those fears down any time they come up.

Before we go any further, think about it. What have your fears kept you from doing?

- Have you ever thought about opening your own business or becoming an entrepreneur, but the potential consequences of financial or emotional catastrophe kept you from making the first move?

- Have the terrifying "what-if's" of approaching attractive girls or guys kept you glued to the wrong side of the room out of fear of rejection or embarrassment, only to leave you lamenting not making your move for the rest of the night when she/he walked past you?

- Are you terrified of getting up in front of co-workers, friends, or even family to give a speech? Has it gotten to the point where you're missing out on career advancements and promotions, or even just saying what's on your mind whenever you feel like it?

- What about things that are a little more extreme? Skydiving? Parasailing? Bungee jumping? Getting that tattoo you've always wanted?

- What about things that are a little less extreme? Strutting up in front of a karaoke crowd to sing that Bon Jovi song you always hum to yourself in the shower? Flying to another country where nobody speaks English? Telling your spouse the truth about something you know will create discomfort between you two, but will ultimately improve your relationship?

Whatever you're afraid of, I would argue that two things are probably true:
1. If you had control over your fears, your life would improve anywhere from "wow...I feel better" to "my life will never be the same and I feel absolutely freaking incredible".
2. You aren't the only one who feels this way.

And because you aren't the only who feels this way, odds are somebody has been through this before. Why? Because ultimately, we all feel fear in relatively similar ways. More on that a little later.

Now, this book is going to uncover several things for you.

First, we're going to look at **how we as a culture avoid risk** and why too many people cruise through life without pushing themselves to go after what they really want. We'll talk about the factors around us that influence our sense of fear, from society to family to your grade school teachers to the commercials we watch on tv.

We'll talk about **taking action to get past those fears**; the three different types of action and **how to implement** each one in your life to create drastic and lasting results.

We'll discuss the **concept of pain**, including how pain can be incredibly motivating and how to use it to your advantage, even when everything in your mind and body is telling you to run the other direction to get away from it.

And throughout the book, I'll be giving you **powerful exercises** along the way that you can implement every day, even if just a couple minutes at a time, to change the way you perceive and react to your fear, and help you to visualize going after the things you really want for yourself.

The bottom line: You have more control over the direction of your life than you can ever imagine, and usually the fears and anxieties that hold you back from taking risks are easier to beat that you think. With a little patience, practice, and pushing yourself, you can learn to tame your own sharks.

(Even literally, if that's your thing.)

Chapter 2:
Meaning and Purpose

Not long ago I had dinner at a sandwich chain here in Austin called *Which Wich*, where you can customize virtually every part of your sandwich. It's a fun concept, too -- they have all the choices of protein, condiments, vegetables, sauces, and other periphery printed out on a brown paper bag, and you use a thick, red Sharpie to select what you want on your sandwich.

You have unending and virtually unlimited power and control over, well...your dinner.

I picked up the bag, wrote out big, bold checkmarks next to each selection for my artichoke-parmesan-provolone sandwich with pesto, 1000 Island, spinach, garlic, and oregano on wheat, wrote my name at the bottom, and walked it up to the young guy behind the counter.

While he was inputting my selections into the register, I noticed the shirt he was wearing. On it, in the standard franchise yellow and black, there was the Which Wich logo, along with a huge empty box in the center.

Above the box, in heavy black capital letters, was written, "THIS YEAR'S GOALS".

The company had obviously had these printed up for their employees, and for some reason, this dude had not done his homework.

I asked him, "Why don't you have any goals on your shirt?" With little more than an embarrassed mumble, he replied, "I dunno...I'll do it next year."

***

I know...I probably wouldn't want to be forced to proclaim my innermost hopes and dreams to every random sandwich chomper either.

But the point was echoed loud and clear: This is a country where we have more choice than we know what to do with. We have a virtually limitless buffet of opportunities in how we make money, in how we choose a mate, in how we can affect other people's lives, etc. But so few of us seize those choices. We coast through life, doing either what we think is expected of us, or doing what we can to make sure the bills get paid.

That's not to say we don't work hard, because many of us do. But how many of us are working out of obligation, as opposed to pursuing our passions?

It amazes me when I see someone so young with a blank box of GOALS. Actually, it baffles me. When I was that age, you could have said to me: "Name 10 goals you have in your life," and I could probably have bounced back triple that for you in less than a minute. I had a fairly clear picture of my "ideal self," even as a kid. I wanted to be in front of people, inspiring and entertaining them, I wanted to make a lot of money so I could travel the world and do fun and amazing things.

Even if you don't have a clear picture of who or what your "ideal self" really is, you more than likely *want* things. And even if that "thing" is as simple as a nice car, or to pull yourself up out of poverty, or to call that hot girl/guy from the marketing department on the phone, that's still something you have not achieved for yourself yet, regardless of what's stopping you from getting it.

If you're living your life without purpose, without inspiration, without yearning for something greater than who your are or what you have now, it's time for some serious thinking. Odds are that you have wanted something bigger for yourself at some point, but somebody or something pushed you down and stopped you from thinking that way.

That doesn't mean those thoughts disappeared. In fact, odds are that they got so squashed, whether through somebody making fun of you or discouraging you, or some element of fear or self doubt.

No matter what it was, it's time you and I get to work.

TIME FOR SOME ACTION:

DIG FOR MEANING AND PASSION

Find a quiet place where you can do some good, solid thinking for at least five minutes. Think about a time in your life when you dreamed of something. Something BIG. Maybe you were five years old and thought of being an astronaut. Maybe you were 20 and wanted to become an investigative journalist. Maybe you wanted to be able to start interesting conversations with random strangers at parties.

And remember...BIG should mean whatever it means to you; not anyone else's definition.

Okay...take 5-10 minutes to think about this. Write notes down if you have to.

And all you're doing is writing down some of those simple wants and desires. This exercise is not about saying how you're going to achieve them or what deterred you from achieving them in the past. Very simply...just write them down in the space here:

_____

_____

_____

Alright...great job. Let's keep moving.

Chapter 3:
Our Perception of Risk

I can still feel Monty, the bright teal parakeet, pressed against my chest. He was shivering and squirming and didn't understand why he wasn't in his cage anymore.

It was a blisteringly cold winter, which was odd for Texas. Temperatures were dangling around 0 degrees. My apartment was quickly losing precious heat, and I needed to keep Monty as warm as I could.

The perpetual white noise of the heater was eerily missing, and even before I woke up, something in me could sense danger. I had awakened about 20 minutes before -- around 6 am. I only knew this by looking at my phone, as the lights on the clock radio had gone dark overnight. I thought maybe the power had gone out. But in the back of my mind, I knew what was really going on.

I had finally reached one of the lowest points in my life. A few months had gone by where I hadn't been able to afford to pay my electric bill, and today was the day my power had been shut off.

Words barely describe the feeling I had that morning. Loser. Hack. My parents would be ashamed of me. I couldn't tell my friends.

My head rattled with the notion that I was a complete, unequivocal failure.

However, that's only one perspective.

The reason I couldn't pay my electric bill was because the business I had started several months back was failing. I wasn't bringing in enough money, and as a result, I couldn't pay my bills.

Being in that position is a scary thing. In fact, it was a major fear of mine. "What if I can't pay my bills?" "What if my electric gets cut off?" It was terrifying, like it meant I was going to freeze to death.

This was the day it actually happened.

But neither Monty nor I froze to death that morning. Truth be told, aside from the temporary embarrassment, shame, and bird bites on my fingers, it wasn't that bad. I was able to cobble together some money and get the bill paid. The lights and the heat came back on. Monty went back in his cage, and I learned how to better prepare for such circumstances.

The point is this: fear keeps us from doing a lot of things. Had I been so paralyzed by fear as to not quit my job and start my business, I would have not had the experience of failing. And what did I learn from getting my lights shut off? It's actually not nearly as bad as I thought it would be.

I'm not suggesting you stop paying your bills just to try it. But making mistakes is part of making things work.

***

Your mind is incredibly powerful. It's constantly working and scheming to protect you, keeping a 24-hour vigil against threats and danger.

However, it's only been over the last few thousand years that we, as a collective species, have outgrown the need for such drastic defenses. 10,000 years ago, there was a good chance that you would turn the corner and come eye to eye with a saber-toothed tiger that had been tracking you for miles and was ready for dinner. As a result, you had to stay constantly aware of whatever may be lurking nearby, setting out the ketchup and mustard in preparation for your arrival.

Fast forward to present day. Although we still face potential destructive events, such as your plane crashing and never being found, falling down a flight of stairs, getting wiped out by the Ebola virus, or getting your head clipped off by the shark you were trying to put into tonic, the chances of those things happening are extremely slim.

In fact, according to the Centers for Disease Control and Prevention (http://www.cdc.gov/nchs/fastats/leading-causes-of-death.htm), you're more likely to die of heart disease, cancer, stroke, or even *suicide* than anything I mentioned above.

Mystery plane crashes didn't even come close to making the top 10 on the CDC's list. So *why* are we still so afraid of such events?

Lots of reasons.

Learning to Avoid Risk: **Cultural Factors**

Tonight's Top Story

Let's flip on the evening news and learn about what happened today in our city.

[click] Oh, look at that...they're leading with a story of a man who was shot and killed. Okay, next story.

[click] Someone else was stabbed and is now on life support. Next.

[click] A fiery, awful car crash. Ouch.

But, at least there's a piece coming up about something crazy that Miley Cyrus did.

Yay.

Your local news (and in many cases, even national news outlets) is typically a lurching death parade of bleak blips that feed us the worst events that happened around us that day. According to an article in *Psychology Today* (http://www.psychologytoday.com/blog/wired-success/201012/why-we-love-bad-news), studies reported that stations air up to seventeen negative news reports for every one good one. We could spend some time exploring *why* this is, as there are plenty of incentives coming from both their viewership and particularly their advertiser base to keep eyeballs glued to the screen. Regardless of the "why," the fact is that news shows us death and peril all day, every day.

It's no wonder we believe we're constantly in mortal danger. We're programmed every day to believe that people are dying around us.

So it's only natural that we don't expose ourselves to that kind of peril.

But let's take another look. Those terrible events, aside from the occasional hijacking, terrorist situation, or mass murder, are limited to a few at a time. Now compare that to the millions upon millions of neutral or positive events that happened on the same day. News outlets have no interest or time to cover those happenings, and nobody would watch them. But the fact is, unless you live or commute to a neighborhood where tragic events happen on a regular basis, the odds are you aren't going to encounter that kind of situation.

I grew up in suburban St. Louis, Missouri. We lived in West County, where everybody lived (and looked) fairly similar. The houses were similar. Cars were similar. Jobs and salaries were similar. And it was a rare day when everything around us wasn't pleasant.

I found the experience fairly vanilla. So when I was old enough to get behind the wheel, I made it a point to begin exploring and experiencing every square inch of that city. I learned, brick by brick, what incredibly rich history surrounded us.

Now if you've been paying attention, you've probably read somewhere that, over the last 10 or 15 years, St. Louis has been consistently ranked in the top 5 most dangerous places in the country. Whenever we turned on the news, there was another report of somebody getting shot and killed.

And admittedly, there are some areas of town that a 16-year old white kid in his dad's white Ford Taurus is ill advised to explore.

But here's the thing; I started finding other people like me who didn't live in West County. They were smart, respectable, great people who had pushed past (or maybe never been exposed to) the stigma that you didn't drive down certain streets. In fact, some of them even *lived* on those streets.

Were they as safe as we were? Maybe not. But no one I know has ever been shot, stabbed, or kidnapped, no matter where in St. Louis they live.

News outlets provide a very pointed and narrow picture of our lives. And if you're really paying attention and looking beyond what you're spoon fed by watching TV or reading the paper, you'll realize that you're not in nearly the danger you're led to believe.

Don't Buy What They're Selling You

Scare tactics in advertising and marketing are nothing new. For years, savvy marketers have worked to induce fear in consumers to motivate us towards hastily pulling out our wallets.

Whether it's depicting young children surrounded by invasive germs to hawk antibacterial soap or showing the effects of a devastating and gruesome wreck because the driver chose a not-as-safe car model, we are being led and influenced by people who have not our best interests, but their bottom lines at heart.

One of the benchmark examples of fearmongering in advertising is the "Daisy" campaign, designed to get Lyndon Johnson elected as president in the mid-1960s. Capitalizing on the Cold War mania of the era, the spot opened with a young girl counting petals of a flower, up from one to nine. Suddenly, an ominous voiceover begins counting back down from 10 to zero, while the camera steadily zooms into one of Daisy's eyes. This segues into footage of a nuclear blast while the voiceover begins spouting rhetoric of how we are headed towards disaster for our children if we don't run out and vote for LBJ.

Although relatively tame compared to what we see now – people getting hit by fast-moving cars, eaten by wild animals, and increasingly bold anti-smoking spots depicting the awful effects of lighting up, "Daisy" perfectly encapsulates the notion that we are very much influenced by advertising and marketing, and that fear is one of the quickest ways to motivate people.

Some researchers argue that fear even trumps sex in motivating buying decisions. In his book *Buyology: Truth and Lies About Why We Buy*, Martin Lindstrom references a study that observed consumers' brains while they are exposed to advertising and specific brands, using functional resonance imaging (fMRI) and electroencephalography (EEG) technology.
(http://www.clickz.com/clickz/column/1692930/neuromarketing-why-fear-sells-sex-doesnt)

The study measured physiological responses, including heart rate, respiratory rate, galvanic skin response and more in a new field coined "neuromarketing." At the close of the study, the researchers concluded that consumers are more motivated by fear than sex, as self preservation is a more primal and foundational need than procreation or pleasure. In other words, it's more important to us to stay alive than to be considered sexually attractive.

Learning to Avoid Risk: *Home*

When I was about six years old, my parents laid down for a nap, leaving me and my sister to play with our toys and entertain ourselves in the living room.

As I rolled and crashed my Transformers over each other, I noticed the USPS mail truck driving by through the blinds. My parents went out to get the mail every day, walking the 14 steps from the front door, down the driveway, to the box, and back in no time. Since they were sleeping, I figured I would take care of it for them.

I opened the door, walked down the driveway. It was a hot St. Louis summer day -- easily over 100 degrees, and the baking asphalt was searing my bare feet. I grabbed the mail, came back and quickly hopped back inside, thinking my burning toes were the limit of that day's discomfort.

When I got through the door, it took my eyes a second to readjust. I scanned the floor for my Transformers, but they were nowhere in sight. They were now obscured by the dark silhouette of my fuming father. He was so angry that I could practically see the steam rising from his ears.

Now in his defense, my dad is not a man prone to yelling or harsh punishment. He is a master at resolving conflict by using intellect over intensity. He's very good at talking and reasoning things out. However, when it comes to the safety of his family, his emotions become a bubbling cauldron.

I could feel the scathing heat looming from only two feet away. His voice bellowed, "What were you doing?!? You NEVER, EVER go outside by yourself!! Do you have any idea what kind of awful people are out there? You could get kidnapped and we would never see you again!"

I recoiled in shock and shame, wondering if all of that was true. My world shrank a little bit, as my childhood sense of invincibility got ripped to shreds, like so much junk mail.

To this day, I still cringe a little when I walk to the mailbox.

***

When you think back to that time in your life, what's the first thing you remember from your parents about risk and danger? Did you try to help make dinner, only to have Mom warn you how you could burn yourself if you weren't careful? Did your parents go through a bankruptcy and you inferred that you were always in danger of going broke? Were you required to sanitize your hands every time you touched a door handle and told you that you were likely to contract the Black Plague if you didn't stay clean?

Perhaps your examples are even more dire than mine. Whatever they are, most kids learn very early on that we are frighteningly vulnerable to lots of bad stuff. Why, there are crazy strangers, drunk drivers, and mouth-foaming rabid animals, every one of them armed with assault rifles, razor teeth, and flu germs and they won't hesitate to kidnap/maul/infect innocent children at the drop of a hat.

At least, that's what our parents wanted us to think. Logically, our parents probably knew that life wasn't quite as dangerous as they were making it out to be for us. But emotionally, they were biologically charged as our protectors. It was their sole responsibility to ensure we made it through childhood as unscathed as possible, and if they failed, the results would be catastrophic.

To our parents, every time we took a figurative (or literal) step forward, it could result in complete and total armageddon. And so, most of us internalized this very early on, decoding the message as "DANGER, DANGER!"

Depending on what you experienced as a kid, we all learned different things about the world. For instance, I used to play in a band with a guy named JJ. JJ has been through virtually everything; he was physically abused by his stepfather. He loves to surf in waters infested with sharks. He had moved to LA and developed, then overcame a heroin addiction. He has traveled all over the world, facing and beating all kinds of danger that would have terrified (or even beaten) most other people.

So what is he afraid of?

When JJ was a kid, his grandfather got sick and wound up in the hospital for a long time. For weeks, he watched as his grandfather, an otherwise strong and powerful person, died slowly and painfully, confined to a sterile, white hospital bed with nowhere to go.

This became JJ's nightmare. He didn't fear the conventional demons that the rest of us do. He learned that the *worst* thing that could happen to him was to get old and sick. So, he has lived his life accordingly, without regret.

***

I would argue that in the typical child-raising scenario, a typical parent tries to get their typical kid into the best school they can find or afford. They push their kid to get good grades, graduate high school (on time) and then go to the best school available. They then go after the best job they can (ideally one that pays them a lot of money), raise a family, and live happily ever after.

In a typical parent's mind, if they can make this dream life a reality, they feel they have succeeded as a parent.

And accordingly, it's rare that a typical parent would encourage their child to follow a life passion at the expense of financial stability. It's counterintuitive to the way a parent is programmed to do their job. You're not a success if you can't pay for groceries or the electric bill.

Of course, this scenario doesn't represent anything close to all parent/child relationships. But as a general rule, parents want their kids to have the safest and most protected life possible.

During that process, we learn to become risk averse. We are taught to avoid thoughts, activities, and pursuits that might make us stray from "the path" (at least from a vocational perspective). And we go on thinking that our fantasies of going after something bigger should remain just that: fantasies.

TIME FOR SOME ACTION:
THE COLD SHOWER

We get used to being comfortable. It feels good to feel good. And it gets to the point where we go out of our way, sometimes WAY out of our way, to avoid feeling uncomfortable.

But the more you push yourself to not only go through that discomfort, but work to move that needle back to "normal" while you're at it, the more you will be able to endure painful situations and do the things you're afraid to do.

Here's one that built up my emotional muscle a few years back. And like most good things, you can do it in the shower.

Start by turning the water on to a comfortable temperature. Start your normal routine in the shower, and stay in there for at least five minutes, until you're comfortable.

Then, step out of the stream of water so that barely any is touching you. Quickly turn the water temperature to the coldest setting possible.

Take a deep breath. Let it out. Then step completely into the stream of cold water.

You will feel physical shock running through your body as your brain sends rapid fire signals to get out of it. Realize, in the moment, that this is all part of conditioning yourself to handle discomfort. You should also begin to feel an endorphin rush, adding to the sensory explosion of the moment.

Stay there as long as you can; shoot for a minimum of 10 seconds. As you get more experienced, go for 30 or even 60 seconds.

During the exercise, talk to yourself in affirmations. "OH YEAH...THIS FEELS GOOD! I'M STRONG! I CAN HANDLE THIS! YEAH!"

When you've had enough, turn the water back to a comfortable temperature.

This exercise really starts to have a lasting, conditioning effect when you perform it several days in a row. So how many days can you handle? Three? Five? A full week? Longer?

No matter how long you stay in the cold water and how many days you complete it, always congratulate yourself for pushing yourself to do something that you knew would make you feel pain, and enduring it.

Chapter 4:

Negative Reinforcement:

It's Not You. It's Me.

Sometimes we are our own worst enemies. Little do we realize that if we accept responsibility for what happens to us, it has the power to change our lives.

Meet Jack. A well-to-do luxury car salesman, he made a multiple six-figure salary. He wore gold rings, and whenever he and his wife Natalie went out to dinner, his demeanor was that of an arrogant sheik. He spoke so the whole place could hear him, and made a habit of ordering servers around like they were his own personal hired help.

Jack and Natalie were living large until one day Jack's boss called him into his office.

He informed Jack that, after several complaints from both customers and fellow employees about his attitude and demeanor, he was no longer a good fit for the company. Jack stormed out of the building and sped home.

"I can't believe this," he said, raging, to his wife. That place is going to fall apart without me. Those idiots just can't take a strong personality; they'll regret it soon enough.

Jack began his search for a new job, but that only took up half the day. With his clout and capabilities, Jack was convinced work was just around the corner. So he felt entitled to spend a little time with the boys and went to the neighborhood pub.

Believing Jack would soon replace his salary as well, Natalie kept spending as she always had, buying pricey clothes, going out to dinner, and enjoying life as though nothing had changed.

The months wore on, and Jack hadn't found a new job. He spent more and more time at the bar, and their savings was dwindling to nothing.

Natalie began to sweat. For the first time in her life, she was feeling desperate and unprepared. Her confidence slowly melted into terror.

One day, after opening a massive credit card statement, she started to panic. Not knowing what else to do, she picked up the phone and called her mom for help.

She pleaded, "We're running out of money, and I'm so scared! I don't know what else to do."

Natalie's mom offered to help them out for a few months while Jack continued to look for a new job. Once again, they had enough money to cover the bills.

For the time being, they could put aside their worries and feel a sense of security again. But instead of using this money as it was intended, Jack kept drinking. And grumbling. He would come home drunk and angry every night, fuming that the company had screwed him over.

A couple months later, Natalie's mom called her daughter to check in on Jack's progress in finding a job.

"Oh, he's trying. But nobody's hiring right now. Plus, no one really appreciates how much he brings to the table. We think it will still be a couple months," she said.

Natalie's mom was no fool. She could sense what was really going on here – that nothing had changed. Jack and Natalie were living the life they always had. In the meantime, they hadn't accepted the reality of what had happened to them, nor accepted responsibility for the situation. They were both convinced it was someone else's fault.

Natalie's mom told her that she could only give them money for another month, but that she wanted to do everything he could to assist Jack in getting another job. She offered hours of her time to build his resume up, go over networking connections, and even take a couple days off to do some cold calling for him. She said, "I bet we could find you something in retail in no time. You would still be in sales, and you could replace your last salary in just a year or two."

Natalie, in a huff, told her she would think about it and hung up the phone. That night she told Jack about the call.

"That's outrageous! She's abandoning us! You don't do that to family," he screamed.

They didn't talk to Natalie's mom for months. Blaming her for leaving them in a lurch, they grew more and angry. In the meantime, their situation didn't improve.

This turned into an ongoing cycle. They would reach a low point and call Natalie's mom to invite her out to lunch. Each time, they found a way to manipulate her into helping them.

When she finally got to a point where she realized this wasn't going to end, she stopped giving them money but offered to help in some other way. And each time, they accused her of being a terrible mother and blamed her for everything that was happening to them.

***

Sound familiar? Do you know someone who thinks this way? Maybe you've even gotten caught up in it the way Allen did; trying to help, but realizing that person isn't likely to change.

We all have times in our lives where we feel a sense of desperation, or that we've been slighted by someone else. And perhaps it's true that you haven't been treated fairly at various points.

But when you spend your life focusing on how others have wronged you, you will never accept responsibility for the situation. This is called having a **victim mentality**, and it's a dead end.

At its core, having a victim mentality is ultimately someone's attempt at having control over a situation when there's none to have. If you can place blame on someone or something, you absolve yourself of any responsibility. You can blame and blame and blame, but realistically, what is that going to get you, aside from a heart full of resentment and a stomach full of ulcers?

And only when you can accept the reality of what has, is, and will happen to you and realize that you are the only one with the power to change it, will you begin to create the change you so desperately want for yourself.

No one can do it for you. You can't blame your way into prosperity or success. It's like waiting to win the lottery in order to pay for groceries. Only when you take accountability for everything that happens to you will to rightfully go after anything you want.

Accepting Responsibility

It's the sign of a very mature person when they are able to accept responsibility for whatever happens to them. Even if someone steals their car, the government takes away their land, or a house falls on their sister, the best thing one can do is understand, "These are the cards I've been dealt. Although it may make me angry or hurt, the best thing I can do is accept the situation as it is, and move on to bigger and better."

The most successful people in the world employ this strategy. When Steve Jobs was fired from Apple, the company he founded, did he sit at home and sulk? Probably for about 20 minutes. Then he went and started NEXT, a company that Apple eventually acquired. And then they came back, begging for him to return.

Even some of the shrewdest business icons in the world have fallen all the way down, and then come back again. Donald Trump has gone bankrupt (four times!), and clawed his way back to the top. Today, he's worth an estimated $3.9 billion dollars (http://www.celebritynetworth.com/richest-businessmen/richest-billionaires/donald-trump-net-worth/) .

I doubt Trump spent much time sitting around sticking needles into voodoo dolls and cursing those who have wronged him. Instead, he accepted that being down is just part of the cycle, and rode it out without losing sight of who was responsible for the outcome of his life: him.

And when you boil it down, responsibility isn't an action; it's a mindset. You don't go through your life angry and playing the victim, change your tune when something goes wrong, and then go back to blaming everybody. People get what they want when they believe in their heart of hearts that they manifested whatever happened to them. They can't control ALL the variables, but they CAN choose how they respond to any particular trigger.

So why waste time, energy, and creativity stewing and plotting revenge? It's counter productive and will likely cause you more anguish than anything else.

How Can I Say This Differently?

Do you talk to yourself? And I don't mean do you walk around with your Bluetooth headset *looking* like you're talking to yourself. Do you actually take the time to tell yourself what you want out of life?

I talk to myself all the time. I learned this technique from a good friend of mine, George. George has made himself and his clients millions of dollars, so I figured it would be wise to listen when he starts talking.

The first thing I do every morning is get out my "Life Optimization" document. It's a list of events and goals I want to achieve in life. I guess some would call it a "Bucket List," but the difference is that these are goals I want to achieve in the next 1-5 years and actively work towards on a daily basis. It's more of a "Life's Navigational Compass" list.

When I first started compiling and line-iteming out these aspirations, I would just write them as I thought of them. Phrases like: "I don't want to have debt anymore." Or "I don't want to work for a boss."

But along the way, I learned a subtle, but very powerful tweak to this strategy.

Tony Robbins, one of my great influences, calls the brain a "servo mechanism." This means it can only do what you tell it to do, and nothing more. Your brain, even though it looks like a big, slimy piece of anatomy, is actually a crazy super machine. With the exception of The Terminator and Johnny 5, machines don't think for themselves. You have to program and tell them what to do. It works like a computer, processing data and working to resolve the problem you give it. But if you provide the wrong data at the beginning of the equation, it processes the problem incorrectly and produces the wrong answer.

When I started conditioning my brain with "I don't want to have debt anymore," I was telling my brain what I didn't want. But I wasn't replacing it with what I *did* want. As a result, my brain didn't know what to work towards.

When I realized this, I changed these affirmations around. They became "I will eliminate all debt within six months" and "I will be self-employed and self-sustaining within one year." (Because, as you know, you have to assign dates to goals to have any chance of achieving them.)

Once I made this change, my goals started going from goals to realities. I eliminated all past debts as a result.

Let's say you want to lose weight. One day you say to yourself, "I don't want to be fat anymore." Then you say it every day for a month.

Congratulations! You've achieved nothing. You've told your brain what you *don't* want. But you haven't told it what you do want.

What if you tried something like, "I want to be thin."

Well, that's a step in the right direction. We've gone from negative to positive. However, you are instructing your brain to *desire* something. You haven't instructed it to work for a desired result, or even condition yourself to believe you are a certain way.

How do you think champion athletes jump or throw or hit or do anything they do as well as they do? They condition themselves to BELIEVE they can do something, even before they can do it. They visualize themselves already able to achieve that feat.

Related back to our diet dilemma, let's reframe again. Instead of *desiring* something, let's already assume we're in that state.

How about, "I am healthy. I look terrific. I eat well, exercise daily, and love who I am. My body is beautiful, and it will continue to bust my ass to get it looking even more slim and trim." And so forth.

Corny? Sure...a bit. But what you're doing is creating alignment in your mind between your current state and your desired state. There's no need to "cross over" and become something you believe you aren't...your brain already believes you're there. You just have to stay on that path, and you'll eventually reach that desired state or condition.

What if you don't? Then you course correct and keep trying until you find something that does work for you.

But it all starts in telling your brain what you are...not what you aren't.

Quieting the Chatterbox

In *Feel the Fear and Do It Anyway*, Susan Jeffers, Ph.D. asserts that we all have a "Chatterbox." Much like it sounds, there's a little speaker in our heads that's constantly squawking at you. It's trying to keep up with everything that's going on, and analyzing and nitpicking away at every...single...thing...in...your...life.

"I'm nervous about this meeting today. Really nervous. I wonder if I wore the right outfit. I know these people are looking for somebody to be assertive, but I wonder if I'm too assertive. Maybe I'm not assertive enough. I wonder how they'll be dressed. I bet I'm underdressed. I wonder if I should have worn the black shoes instead of these brown ones. Those brown ones really aren't as nice as these are. But these aren't even that nice. I wonder if I have time to go buy new shoes before this meeting. I bet I could make it if I hurry. But that might make me late. I was late those couple times and my boss didn't say anything, but I know he was thinking about it. He hates it when people are late. I wonder if he thinks I'm late all the time. I hope I don't get fired. I don't know what I would do if I get fired. If I had to, I could start freelancing. I bet I'd be good at that. But who would hire me? There are so many people working cheaper than I do."

All that self talk, all that worry...it can drive you NUTS. But for most of us, our Chatterbox is almost always on. It's a circular mechanism that just seems to keep reinforcing the negative thoughts that flood your mind on a daily, if not hourly basis.

So, what do you do about it?

1. **First, awareness is key.** Catch yourself next time it happens. Hold that thought in your head, the same way you would hold a lightning bug before letting it flap away. Be aware that it's there.

2. **Next, take a moment to analyze that thought or concern.** Is this a valid and realistic worry? Or are just worrying out of habit and fear? For instance, will wearing the wrong color shoes really cost you a new account? Or are you just

worrying out of habit?

3. **Practice breathing.** Thích Nhất Hạnh, a renowned Vietnamese Zen Buddhist monk, teacher, and author, asserts that virtually any worry can be addressed by taking the time to breathe with it. It's a deceptively simple practice that can yield some massive results, for two reasons. First, by focusing on your breathing, you are refocusing your mind, which squeezes out the other chaotic thoughts and fears. Simple breaths in, and simple breaths out. Second, you are changing your physiological state. When we are panicked, we take small, quick breaths. We developed this along our evolutionary lines because taking shorter breaths prepares us for action, like to evade a predator. However long, deep breaths tell our nervous systems that all is well and that it's time to calm down. More on this later.

I Can't Change. I Don't Know How.

There have been a new crop of web-based brain exercise tools popping up over the last few years. One is Lumosity.com. They consist of small, simple, and repetitive exercises that push your mental muscle just an inch or two at a time.

These tools work on the principle of *Neuroplasticity*.

Up until even a few decades ago, scientists thought that the brain was static. In other words, it was believed that, once you reach adulthood, your brain doesn't change much in composition, and if ever damaged, it stays that way and can't heal itself.

Neuroplasticity challenged this notion. Scientists have proven that your brain is a dynamic organ, constantly making new synaptic connections and creating fresh neural pathways based on how you

train it. There have even been cases of stroke patients with brain damage, who were unable to speak or even walk after the incident, regaining the ability to do both even months after it happened. This only happens through simple and consistent action.
(http://www.amazon.com/Brain-That-Changes-Itself-Frontiers/dp/0143113100/ref=sr_1_3?s=books&ie=UTF8&qid=1407630793&sr=1-3&keywords=neuroplasticity)
What this means for us is that when you *learn* you need to be afraid of something, your brain is physiologically reinforcing that notion. It's almost like when a city starts building higher levies after a devastating hurricane. Once something feels scary, your brain is actually building new pathways to better protect you.

But what if we looked at this from the other side? When you learn how to overcome a fear, and do so consistently over time, your brain paves that new neural road as well. That's why confidence is like dominos; it's hard to get a little at first, but a little begets a little more, which begets a little more.

Keep this in "mind" as you work to overcome fears and build confidence -- that your brain is backing you up, for better or for worse, every step of the way.

TIME FOR SOME ACTION:
CHALLENGING YOUR "I AM's"

If you've never seen or read *Fight Club*, it's a great study in what you can do when you let go of the living in the confines of your "self."

The book's main character is a white, upper class guy with a high-paying job who has no direction or meaning to his life. He focuses on wanting and needing insignificant material goods, because he has nothing else to really want. He feels empty and purposeless, and begins to search outside himself for answers.

WARNING: SEMI-SPOILER ALERT. SORRY.

Sure, there are lots of stories like that. But where *Fight Club* takes a turn is when the lead character invents a persona to achieve tasks he would normally never even dream of doing. When he's in this other character, he's an athlete, a leader, a god even. He pushes every boundary and law and liquor store he can knock over. More importantly, he pushes his own ideology. He completely steamrolls the way he lives his life and lives without consequence or fear of what people think about him or how his actions affect others.

I'm leaving a lot out here, just in case you want to see it. As you should.

So, what if you were that character? What if you woke up tomorrow and suddenly, every little thing that holds you back from doing what you want to do had vanished? You no longer cared if people thought you looked a fool. You took action without fear of running out of money. You pursued the person you're most attracted to without any thought of rejection.

Based on our experiences, circumstances, and habits, each one of us believes that we embody a very specific, unchangeable identity.

"I'm conservative -- I don't take risks."

"I only look good in navy blue."

"I'm analytical, so I can only do analytical work."

It's natural to take on those beliefs -- they help craft your identity, whether you want them to or not. We believe: I AM a systems analyst. I AM a devoted wife and mother and could never leave. I AM a devout follower of my faith.

But...what if you weren't?

Try this...make a list of things that describe you. It can include anything -- just things that you "are."

Then next to every word, write the opposite.
For example:

Christian	Atheist
Analytical	Creative
Staunch Conservative	Flaming Liberal
Careful	Crazy Risk Taker

See how many you can do.

The point of the exercise is this: you become who you are for various reasons, and sometimes you don't even know that you've become that person. Even further, you're unhappy because of your identity, but you don't even really know what elements comprise that identity.

This is an exercise to learn more about yourself, what motivates you, and what you can start to do at a fundamental, down-deep level to begin to change those beliefs. It can be a slow and at times uncomfortable process, but in the end you will know yourself better. And by knowing what you believe about yourself, you can start to make the changes you really want to make in your life.

Now get to it.

BONUS MINI-MISSION: UNBROKEN EYE CONTACT

Just how comfortable are you with eye contact?

A few years ago, my friend Ryan and I started a small men's group. We would meet once a week and constantly challenge each other to become better men and better humans.

We would use specific activities in the group to build trust and camaraderie. This was one of them.

Try this.

With a friend, co-worker, or family member, find a quiet place where you won't be disturbed for about 10 minutes. Set up two chairs facing each other, or stand about a foot or two apart.

Take a moment to relax, then begin staring directly into each others' eyes.

Keep in mind that this is not a contest to see who will blink first. There isn't supposed to be a winner or loser. The goal is simply to get past any discomfort associated with making prolonged eye contact.

You both might smile, giggle, or look away every so often. But when that happens, simply come back to center and look into the middle of the other person's eyes for as long as possible.

What do you notice about the other person? Their facial expressions. The details around that part of their face?

What feelings come up for you? How difficult is it to maintain eye contact?

Start with a couple minutes if possible, and work your way up to 8 or 10 over time. You'll notice that practicing this way will make it easier to look other people in the eye as well.

Chapter 5:
Our Vulnerabilities to Fear

"If you're wondering whether or not you're an addict, you might be one. Just allow yourself the time to listen to us share about what it has been like for us. Perhaps you will hear something that sounds familiar to you. It doesn't matter whether or not you have used the same drugs others mention. It is not important which drugs you used; you're welcome here if you want to stop using. Most addicts experience very similar feelings, and it is in focusing on our similarities, rather than our differences, that we are helpful to one another."

-Welcome to Narcotics Anonymous *booklet*

I had only heard of Steve Mayeda when I invited him to come to my recording studio. I was interviewing influential change makers for the first incarnation of *Courage, Inc.*, a membership site I built to encourage others to begin overcoming fears.

Steve had a reputation around Central Texas for being able to help any guy be able to push past his doubts and insecurities and approach, meet, and woo any woman he wanted. So, I was curious to learn the magic behind the curtain.

When we were first scheduling the interview, he told me he was only going to be in town for one night that week and had another meeting on the books. But he invited me to join him...without telling me where we were headed.

Before the meeting we met up for dinner at a local place around 8 pm called 24 Diner. I sat down and offered to buy us both a round of drinks.

"Actually," he said, "I don't drink. But you're welcome to go ahead."

I wanted to be respectful, so I declined. We started chatting.

"So, you said you had another meeting tonight. Is this related to your coaching business?" I inquired.

"No," he replied. "It's a *Narcotics Anonymous* meeting. I drive in from Dallas once a week to attend."

Uhh...what? What had I signed up for here?

We got through dinner and I hopped in his car. A few minutes later, we arrived at the church where they were holding the meeting. Feeling fairly out of my element, I followed him inside and into a room that was roughly 15 x 10, with barely enough room to move around. The stark white, cinder block walls had been painted over several times since the place had been built and were covered up by various posters and flags, introducing some color and warmth into an otherwise barren and desolate place.

It was a stuffy Austin evening, and the dense summer humidity was choking the air around my face and neck. My eyes quickly darted around the room; there were 7 or 8 people in a circle, tucked onto the kinds of tattered chairs and ragged, cramped couches that had seen some rough times, but now had a second life in this room.

I peered into the faces of the people in the room as we took our seats. Cold and empty, but with a strange presence and energy.

This kind of gathering was completely new to me, and it took me off guard. This was not a networking group, with each attendee there only to advertise their own business, collect cards, and move on to the next meeting. Every person in that room appeared as though they had spent all day cobbling together the emotional strength and courage to get in the car and, pun fully intended, "come to Jesus." They all were there in that stuffy church closet with towering purpose and intent. They were each fighting their own war, all with a common enemy, and that enemy could never be fully beaten. In some ways, that enemy was themselves.

The host introduced himself and launched into what was obviously a scripted monologue that I supposed every host of every group around the country was saying to his or her members that night. It was the same script that was used every week.

Hello, I'm an addict and my name is ____. Welcome to the _____ group of Narcotics Anonymous. Can we open this meeting with a moment of silence for the addict who still suffers, followed by the **WE** *version of the Serenity Prayer.*

The meeting progressed and we went around the circle, one by one. I was nervous, as an outsider who had never done any hard drugs before, that I would be scorned or looked down upon. I could barely comprehend where I was, let alone understand the fight that these people had to endure every single day of their lives. But when it came my turn to speak, I introduced myself very simply and explained how Steve had invited me. I finished with a tentative "thank you for having me here" and sat back in my stiff, green-and-white plaid chair. I waited for the response, not knowing what would happen. Some people smiled, some looked away, and some even said "thank you" back to me.

But what happened next would change my life.

I looked harder and deeper into those faces around the circle. Virtually ALL of them, even the ones who weren't looking at me, seemed to share a sense of knowing, like they could all see something about me that was completely familiar...almost like they knew I was fighting a similar war.

I didn't get it at the time. But reflecting back on that dark night, it was like I was peering into eight glimmering mirrors.

I listened to the stories, one by one. With each one it felt like I was being handed a pile of hardened bricks to hold in my lap, the story of the struggle of each addiction weighing me down to the floor.

By the time the meeting was over and we left, I was exhausted. I still had to do the interview with Steve, but I couldn't get past the shift that had just taken place.

I had never realized it before that night, but I had an addiction.

***

I can't claim that my own struggles come anywhere close to the same zip code as the members of that group. But what I got from that meeting, more than anything, was the sense of the great lengths I went to in order to avoid feeling pain. Gorging myself on fatty foods, pursuing women, spending hours talking to strangers online; I would later learn that they all resulted in the same neurochemical cocktail that illicit drugs do; the release of dopamine.

Dopamine is a chemical released in the brain when we achieve a particular goal. They come in bursts, make us feel great, and are extremely addictive. In his fantastic book, *Leaders Eat Last*, author and speaker Simon Sinek explains that as we evolved over thousands of years, food was scarce and we had to do everything we could to survive. So when we saw something like an apple tree off in the distance, we involuntarily gave ourselves a shot of dopamine in order to encourage ourselves to keep going after those apples. The closer we got, the more dopamine we received, until we finally arrived and stuffed ourselves silly.

Fast forward to present day. Food is no longer scarce, and survival is a heck of a lot easier than it used to be. But we have a whole new set of circumstances. In my own life, combine a healthy dose of adolescent social awkwardness with budding identity issues, along with a little splash of undiagnosed ADD, and my childhood was rife with pleasure seeking (read: dopamine releasing) activities whenever I could get my brain's hands on them.

And although drugs and alcohol were never a major part of that cocktail, I still pushed these other activities to excess because they made me feel better. And when I didn't engage in them, my emotional fuel gauge was on "E." I craved them. I sacrificed relationships and friendships and people's feelings (and trust) so I could get a fix.

And nothing ever had a lasting effect or got better.

***

I go back to that phrase from the beginning of the chapter:

"Most addicts experience very similar feelings, and it is in focusing on our similarities, rather than our differences, that we are helpful to one another."

Most of us would never consider ourselves addicts. We don't jab needles in our arms, sniff powders up our noses, and most of us limit our drinking to social events.

But…Have you ever stopped to consider that you might be using things like food, sex, or your phone, tablet, laptop, gaming console, or TV to escape the fears pervading your life?

The Center for Internet and Technology Addiction (http://virtual-addiction.com) exists specifically to address these growing e-vices, and they mean business.

On their website are several "tests" that measure just how addicted you may be to your devices. On the "Smartphone Abuse Test" page, it reads:

The popularity of smartphones has increased greatly over the past five years. Although their convenience and powerful capabilities are undeniable, many people spend too much time using them or get distracted by them, neglecting healthy "real-time" presence or deeper interpersonal contact. This short quiz will help you to determine if your smartphone use has gotten out of hand, adversely affected your productivity, or created an imbalance in your personal or family life.

1. Do you find yourself spending more time on your Smartphone than you realize?
Yes or No

2. Do you find yourself mindlessly passing time on a regular basis by staring at your Smartphone even when there might be better or more productive things to do?
Yes or No

3. Do you seem to lose track of time when on your Smartphone?
Yes or No

4. Do you find yourself spending more time with Texting, Tweeting, or Emailing as opposed to talking to real-time people?
Yes or No

5. Has the amount of time you spend on your Smartphone been increasing?
Yes or No

6. Do you secretly wish you could be a little less wired or connected to your Smartphone?
Yes or No

7. Do you sleep with your Smartphone ON under your pillow or next to your bed regularly?
Yes or No

8. Do you find yourself viewing and answering Texts, Tweets, and Emails at all hours of the day and night—even when it means interrupting other things you are doing?
Yes or No

9. Do you Text, Email, Tweet or Surf while driving or doing other similar activities that require your focused attention and concentration.
Yes or No

10. Do you feel your use of Smartphones actually decreases your productivity at times?
Yes or No

11. Do you feel reluctant to be without your Smartphone, even for a short time?
Yes or No

12. When you leave the house you ALWAYS have your Smartphone with you and you feel ill-at-ease or uncomfortable when you accidentally leave your Smartphone in the car or at home, or you have no service, or it is broken?
Yes or No

13. When you eat meals is your Smartphone always part of the table place setting?

Yes or No

14. When your phone rings, beeps, buzzes do you feel an intense urge to check for texts, tweets or emails, updates, etc.?
Yes or No

15. Do you find yourself mindlessly checking your phone many times a day even when you know there is likely nothing new or important to see?
Yes or No

***

These kinds of addictions may not be as pervasive or damaging as narcotics or alcohol. But they might also be keeping you from facing your fears and anxieties, as they have with me.

As with most disorders, the first step is awareness. Know that you're engaging in behaviors to avoid feeling the realities of what's going on in your life. Then, you can start to hack away at the real problem, one step at a time.

So, what are you avoiding? And what are you doing to avoid it?

The Science of Fear: Take the High Road

There are several parts of your brain that work together while assessing a potential threat. They work in concert with each other to determine whether you're in danger, and if so, produce a fear response to motivate you to get outta Dodge.

So let's run through what typically happens when you encounter a threat to your safety. And just for fun, let's call that threat, "Gigantic, ominous, dark shadow quickly approaching you in the open ocean."

Here's what happens.

First, meet the thalamus. The thalamus acts as a sort of scout that observes and absorbs external information. (http://en.wikipedia.org/wiki/Thalamus) Its job is to regulate sleep, consciousness, and alertness. But most importantly, it relays sensory signals to the appropriate locations. So when your eyeballs notice a "Gigantic, ominous, dark shadow quickly approaching you in the open ocean," it radios ahead and says, "Hey -- you might want to check this out."

That signal is picked up by the amygdala, which is roughly the size and shape of an almond. The amygdala is responsible for receiving and decoding the messages from sensory receptors all over your body; visuals, smells, sounds, and so forth. It then helps turn that information into a particular bodily response, like fear or anger, to help you decide what to do next.
(http://neuroscience.uth.tmc.edu/s4/chapter06.html)

Finally, that message gets beamed over to the hypothalamus. This organ acts as the "on/off switch" for fight or flight response. It decides whether you're going to run for the hills.

You can compare this to a submarine, like the one in the movie *Crimson Tide*. The thalamus is like the radar room where they receive signals about enemy boats, the amygdala is the control room (the con) where they collect all the information about what's going on, and the hypothalamus is like Captain Ramsey, who makes the decision on how to handle the situation. (Although you could argue that for half the movie, the hypothalamus is more like Lt. Commander Hunter, because he has the Captain locked in his stateroom and assumes command for violating naval rules governing strategic nuclear missile launch. Terrific movie.)

So, that's how most animals process a threat as it's happening. However a number of years ago, Joseph E. LeDoux, Ph.D., a professor of neuroscience and psychology at New York University and director of the Center for the Neuroscience of Fear and Anxiety, discovered that there was another pathway that fear could take through your brain, if you gave it a little extra time and thought. (http://www.cns.nyu.edu/labs/ledouxlab/overview.htm)

He concluded that, instead of transmitting the message directly from the amygdala to the hypothalamus to begin the fight or flight response, that more highly-evolved creatures take the time to run it through the hippocampus first. Your hippocampus stores and receives conscious memories, and then establishes context for what's going on instead of just reacting. He calls this the **High Road Fear Response**. By taking this extra step, you are using your past memories and general knowledge of the world to determine whether this is a true threat, or if you're okay to turn off the alarm system. It helps you distinguish whether that loud knock at the door is a 9-foot burglar holding a shotgun who's about to pound the door down, or just the FedEx guy here to deliver your *Saved By The Bell* box set that was scheduled to arrive today.

And this being the High Road, the response I described earlier without the involvement of the hippocampus Ledoux deemed the **Low Road Fear Response**.

So getting back to our example…let's say you've just now seen the gigantic, ominous, dark shadow quickly approaching you in the open ocean. The Low Road Response would lead you to almost immediately jump into panic, thinking to yourself, "It's Megalodon, the prehistoric 50-foot monster shark! He's back from extinction and here to swallow me whole! Turn around now!"

However, using the High Road Response, you quickly think back to when you were here in these same waters last summer. You remember your tour guide telling you that massive schools of tuna tend to cluster together this time of year and move as though they were one, big unit. You realize that there's no threat at all, and that the return of Megalodon is just as farcical as Bigfoot, U.F.O.s, or a well-written Justin Bieber song.

Now, what's the point of our little tour around your skull?

The High Road Fear Response is not necessarily a completely voluntary body reaction. Fear responses depend on a number of different factors, including but not limited to how much scary stimuli are happening at once, your mental or physiological state in the moment, how much coffee you've had that day, etc.

However, you now know how your brain processes information and you become afraid. And you now know that, by trying to build a little context into the situation and *think* about what's going on instead of just freaking out and looking for an escape hatch, you can begin to gain more control over your fears instead of letting them control you. In other words, *don't panic*.

DID YOU KNOW...

The human body's response to fear and anxiety (or stress) is exactly the same whether a threat is real or imagined. That's why we like roller coasters so much; we get the same endorphin rush as if we were in real danger, but can enjoy it because we know there are few to no real world consequences.

TIME FOR SOME ACTION:
YOUR GREATEST HITS

If your life had a "Greatest Hits" compilation album, what would be on it?

Think about what you've achieved in your life that you're proud of. *Really* proud of. Look back on achievements when you've pushed yourself harder than ever before, events that have defined your character.

The average album has around 10-15 tracks. Yours should too, even if you have to reach a bit to get them. Don't worry if some of your "tracks" aren't as significant as others. But if it had a significant bearing on your life, put it in there.

Examples: "When I walked across the stage at graduation." "When I got my first job." "When I rescued the dog from my neighbor's burning house." "When I left my abusive husband." "When I approached the most beautiful woman in the entire room and asked for her number."

So, what does your *"Greatest Hits"* album look like?

_____

_____

_____

_____

_____

_____

BONUS MINI-MISSION: PROGRESSIVE STRANGER PERMISSIONS

One of my favorite games is to see what I can talk random strangers into doing. Not weird, freaky, or manipulative stuff, but working to push the boundaries of social norms and conventions in order to have a real, human experience with somebody you would otherwise not even stop to even make eye contact with.

For about a year, I sold high-priced blenders in places like Whole Foods and Costco. These are stores where shoppers don't come to chit chat, and even conversations with the people handing out samples are traditionally limited to an awkward smile or empty "thank you."

My job was to disrupt this pattern in those who passed by my booth so they would stop to pay attention. But, you have to give people a reason to pay attention. You do this by challenging their normal patterns of comfortable habit.

My most reliable "bit" was, as someone would be passing by, ask them how they were doing. Nine times out of 10, the response was inevitably something like, "Fine. How are you?"

And because convention and habit dictate that we are supposed to respond with something reciprocally positive and innocuous like, "I'm good," I would respond with the opposite.

I would raise my voice and proclaim, "TERRIBLE!"

This would of course get the person to stop and look at me, and many would even ask, "Why -- what's wrong?" Mission accomplished: I had now laid the groundwork for a real conversation, because I had snapped them out of their existing frame of mind and into our shared present reality.

I use this technique even when I'm not trying to sell anything, but when I want to see what kind of authentic response I can elicit from someone. Why? Because we're all people, we all have things to teach and learn from each other, and you never know how someone you've never met before could impact your day, or perhaps even change your life.

So, here's your mission:
STEP 1: Start talking to strangers.

Next time you're in a grocery store, shopping for electronics, in line to get your morning bagel, etc., start talking. It doesn't matter what you say. Just talk. Try to disrupt the patterns we're used to and have a real, authentic conversation.

If you're not used to initiating conversations with strangers, this will feel really uncomfortable at first. You will think you're bothering people, or that you might even get yelled at. And sure, that possibility is there. It *has* happened to me before.

So what if you do? First of all, you'll get over it, especially if you keep practicing. And second, what if the person you're "bothering" actually WANTS to talk with you? Maybe they're bored, lonely, or think what you're doing is interesting. What if it works?

Now what?

STEP 2: Graduated permissions.
Not long ago I was out on a rooftop bar in downtown Austin with two friends. We were standing around when a couple who we would find out was from out of town, stepped up to the bar to order a drink. After talking for a few minutes, we all decided to move on to the next bar together. When we got there, we found and engaged

another couple (who were easily in their 50s or 60s). All seven of us were sharing drinks, stories, and by the end of the night, the older couple was trying to fix me up with their daughter over the phone.

How far can you take a new connection? Can you get a handshake? A hug? Can you set a business meeting? Can you immediately go get coffee together?

Even better, what if you've connected enough to create your own secret handshake or inside joke that's exclusive only to you?

Start talking to strangers and see how far you can take it. You never know when a random person could become your new best friend.

Chapter 6:

Action & Motivation

"People often say that motivation doesn't last. Well, neither does bathing. That's why we recommend it daily."

-Zig Ziglar

A couple years ago I was at a conference where I stepped into a session about the notion of "bootstrapping a business." 90 minutes later, my concept of being an entrepreneur had totally changed.

The presenter, Bijoy Goswami, outlined not just what "bootstrapping" meant and how that term came to be, but how the mindset of bootstrapping had shaped our country. He even claimed that America is the biggest bootstrap project of all time, as it has been shaped by forces that weren't planned ahead of time.

As Bijoy explained it, you have essentially two choices when starting a business (or any new life endeavor). You either have a lot of money and not much time, like in the case of getting money from investors or a hedge fund, or you have not much money but *a ton of time*. That's where bootstrapping begins.

Bootstrapping is the process of starting and growing a business (or any endeavor) through a series of learning experiences, which some people "mistakenly" call mistakes. It's a combination of luck, timing, and the emotional tenacity to learn from every misstep and rejection. You have to look at failures as learning experiences that ultimately help you improve the business.

Some of the biggest companies and most inspiring people in history bootstrapped their way to new inventions or concepts. But rarely did they ever do this on the first try.

One of my favorite billboards I've ever seen featured a picture of Thomas Edison, who invented the light bulb. The caption reads, *"And on the 10,000th try, there was light."*

Imagine if he had given up on the first try. Or even the 9,999th try. We would all be in the dark.

Bootstrapping a business is about bumbling your way through missteps and failures in order to figure out what is going to make that business work. During that process, you are actually shaping the character and identity of the business. Again, this can apply to anything you're working to achieve in your life. Some people call it "hacking" your life or brain.

However, taking this approach of moving forward without a map takes both consistent motivation and perpetual action. You have to not only maintain a mindset that you will find solutions to any and all challenges you face, but you have to have to keep up the courage and tenacity to keep moving, every day, in order to find those solutions.

So, let's talk about different types of motivation and action.

***

We learned in the last couple chapters that positive self talk is one of the most important tools you have. "The story" you tell yourself has more bearing on your success than virtually any other factor. Support, timing, opportunities, luck, and skill are worthless if you aren't convinced you will find a way to make things happen, and this is true with virtually any endeavor; whether personal or professional.

And to keep that concept at the front of your mind, I believe in three types of motivation, all of equal power and importance.

3 Types of Motivation

1. **Conscious**:
   Conscious motivation involves the act of physically or mentally telling yourself, "I can do this!" You can communicate this to yourself through verbal affirmations, little notes to yourself, looking in the mirror while pounding on your chest and hollering at the top of your lungs, and so forth. It's doing something to convince or remind yourself that you have the potential, skills, and deservedness to achieve whatever it is you want.

2. **Unconscious**:
   Unconscious motivation is the opposite of negative self talk and conditioning. When you start believing in yourself and developing confidence, it tends to snowball. This typically only happens after you've both properly motivated yourself, as described in Action Type #1, as well as what we're about to talk about in Action Type #3.

   When I was younger, I used to have dreams that I was about to get in a fight. In each dream, I would square off with someone bigger than me, and I started to throw a punch. But when I went to land it on the other guy, everything from my arm down to my hand would turn to jelly and the entire scene would slow down so that I was barely moving. That would obviously have no effect on my opponent, and I would spend the rest of my dream getting pummeled. Not a fun way to wake up the next morning.

   When I was in my mid-twenties, I started lifting weights and putting on a lot of muscle. Not only could I see a difference in my physique, but I could feel it in the way I moved and carried myself. After a month or two of this routine, one night I had another dream. The set up was the same as before -- I was being taunted by some guy, and he tried to push me. Without warning, I threw a punch so hard that it immediately knocked him to the ground and he was out. The fight was over, and I'd totally won without even trying.

I woke up the next morning and realized I was glowing. My entire mentality had shifted, and I felt a sense of physical confidence that had never been there before. As a result, I became much less afraid of confrontation, and was motivated to push myself even harder and risk in other areas of my life.

3. **Movement:**

    Movement motivation comes from getting out of your head and DOING. You stop thinking about how to achieve something, and just start taking the steps to make it happen. You may or may not have support or a plan, but you are starting to move anyway. If you have a fear of heights, you climb up the high dive and jump off anyway.

    This type of motivation is *extremely* powerful, yet it's the hardest kind to get. It involves manually overriding all your internal alarms and warning systems and being uncomfortable. But it also yields the biggest results, as you are beginning to accept the risks of the situation, and as Susan Jeffers, Ph.D. says, "Feeling the fear and doing it anyway." In doing so, you reprogram your mind, affecting the High Road Fear Response by providing stronger context for when future fears pop up, as well as lay new pathways in your brain thanks to neuroplasticity.

3 Types of Action

Movement motivation (from above) is a type of action. It involves moving from *thinking* about making a change to *taking actual steps* towards that change. Just like motivation itself, there are various ways you can take action. And I believe there's a place for each.

Type of Action #1: Eventual Osmosis
Speed: Slow

This type of action is about putting small amounts of consistent, deliberate energy towards solving a problem, overcoming a fear, and/or achieving a goal. It's when you work towards change a little bit at a time so that you can better understand the realities of your situation and course correct as you move forward.

I used to work with a cognitive therapist who believed in this kind of approach. It was rare that he ever gave me assignments, tools to use, or things to try. Instead, we would meet once a week, and he would allow me to talk, almost to the point of free association. This gave me the chance to get anything off my chest. Every now and then, he would ask me a question to get me thinking in a particular direction.

To me, it was agonizingly slow. I tend to work best by doing homework assignments that yield fast results, like our "Time For Some Action" exercises contained in this book. Instead, he allowed me to reach realizations an inch at a time until they eventually, at the speed of molasses, got me to larger insights and epiphanies.

And to his credit, it worked. I started noticing subtle-yet-powerful shifts in my thinking and behavior, feeling like I'd developed some powerful tools to handle situations I'd previously ignored.

However, there's a downside to this approach that you should be aware of. There's a concept you may have heard of called "**analysis paralysis.**" Essentially, it happens when you think, cogitate, and mull things over so much that you never take action because you don't know where or how to start, or that you're afraid you're going to screw it up. Eventual Osmosis involves using your head, and keep in mind that you should, sooner than later, begin using your hands and feet. If you're going to employ this method, give yourself some accountability steps, right from the beginning, to hold your feet to the fire and make sure that you're actually moving towards overcoming your fears.

Type of Action #2: MASSIVE
Speed: Fast

Massive Action involves just that -- taking GIANT steps towards overcoming a fear or achieving a goal. It's what Movement Motivation is all about: casting fear aside and just *doing*, despite whatever pain or consequences arise as a result.

This is an extremely powerful action mode, as you are no longer focused on what could go wrong. You're not subconsciously trying to talk yourself out of it in order to avoid the pain that will arise. Instead, you're accepting that there will be pain as you push out of your comfort zone.

I call this time when you feel discomfort the "**Initiation Period**." You don't feel comfortable because you're adjusting to this new state, and that adjustment sucks. But there's a higher sense of self that's calling the shots, and you're rolling the dice that the benefits from taking Massive Action will outweigh the discomfort you feel during the Initiation Period.

There's a nature spot here in Austin called Hamilton Pool. It's a natural spring formation that stretches about 30 feet across, and at its deepest, is probably 10-15 feet down. Its backdrop is a massive rock grotto that encompasses the scene in a 1,000-foot round, circular, cave-like overhang, and then stretches up a good 60 or 70 feet to a cliff. Beautiful place.

On hot days (of which we get a lot), it's customary for visitors to take a dip in the pool. However, there's one caveat...

The water is ice-freaking cold.

On typical Texas days, the water is a relief from the oppressive heat. However, I happened to be there on a day when it wasn't as hot outside, making the water even colder.

As I dipped a toe into the water, an emotional chill swept over me. It was SO cold. I was not looking forward to the next five minutes.

I realized very quickly that I had two choices. I could, A) Do this one limb at a time, allowing myself to feel that chill little by little, in a prolonged, but controlled exposure.

Or B), I could rip off the band-aid, and just jump in.

But that's it, isn't it? I was afraid, because I was anticipating how much pain and discomfort was about to hit my body. The anticipation of feeling pain kept me in my head, which kept me from taking the leap.

Finally, I made the decision and jumped. Just then, I felt a chilling, frosty torture as my body worked to adjust to the sudden shock.

But, after about 15 seconds, I did adjust. And the fear was gone. It was suddenly completely worth the "Initiation Period" where I felt the pain. Then, I was fine.

One comment about Massive Action...sometimes we get excited and super motivated and try to take on too much at once, at which point we begin to feel overwhelmed. This is not uncommon, and happens often when you're biting off a big problem.

But, just like when you bite off more food than you can chew, the solution is to back up and break things into chunks. You look at what you can do to take things one step at a time while maintaining strong, bold, and consistent action. It's equally as powerful.

Type of Action #3: HABITS & ROUTINE
Speed: Moderate

This is the the balanced approach between Types 1 and 2. With Habits & Routine, you spend time planning and creating clear goals and objectives. You plan for actions you can perform, every day, to help you achieve that goal or beat that fear. Then, you do it, staying true to that plan. Every single day.

This approach requires the highest level of discipline, because there is no adrenaline rush from taking Massive Action, nor the comfort of slowly flowing into it with the Eventual Osmosis technique. However, it typically results in the biggest payoff. As the saying goes, "Slow and steady wins the race."

A couple years ago, my friend Katie wanted to lose 100 lbs. She didn't want to go on a crash or fad diet, nor did she want it to take years.

Katie is a great solver of problems. So, she attacked this one the same way she would anything else. She started by doing her research. She sought out others who had lost 100 lbs. or more, and interviewed each one.

After speaking with enough of these success stories to find the patterns and overlapping points, she developed a plan that she would stick to every day. She followed it to the letter. And after several months, she had shed all 100 lbs. She looks and feels completely different, and to this day she's kept it off.

All three of these Types of Action can work for you, depending on the application. If in doubt, start slow. But if/when baby steps aren't yielding the results you want, use giant steps and accept that there will be some discomfort. And in that situation, the best thing you can do is to remind yourself, every day, that you will be a better person on the other side of that dark tunnel.

TIME FOR SOME ACTION:
LET'S BUILD YOUR PLAN

Get out a sheet of paper, turn it sideways, and draw four vertical columns. At the top of the first one, write, "I'm Afraid Of...". Leave the other three empty.

Then, take a few minutes and list your biggest fears. I'm not talking about nuclear disaster, getting hit by cars, becoming engulfed by Sharknadoes, or the like. Let's keep this to real stuff that you want to do but have been too afraid.

For example, maybe it's starting your own business. Maybe you have a boss and haven't wanted to speak up during meetings. Perhaps you have wanted to travel, but are afraid you will lose your passport, get robbed, and have no way home.

No matter what it is, write down at least 5-10 fears.

Now in the second column, write at the top: "What Could Happen?" Then, write down what you're afraid of happening. Losing your job. Your spouse leaving you. And so forth. Don't be afraid to search your mind for the biggest fear you have surrounding that action.

Now in the third column, write down, "What Will Realistically Happen?" If you were to speak up during that meeting, are you *realistically* going to lose your job? Or realistically, are people maybe going to say something a little insulting and move on?

If you walk across the room to talk to that stranger, are they *realistically* going to throw a drink in your face and slap and scream at you? 9 times out of 10, the answers in this column, if you approach it the right way, will be far less scary than what's happening in column 2.

Now finally, in Column 4, write this: "Level of Future Regret?"

This one is a little tougher. Think about your life a year from now. 5 years. 10 years.

Picture yourself near the end of your life. You were too afraid to do that thing several years ago; how do you feel about it now? Does it seem like you weren't being true to yourself, and that you were simply reacting to a series of impulses that could have simply been overcome?

Now come back to the moment, and write a number. 1 means you won't regret it at all. 10 means you are going to be miserable for the rest of your life if you don't take action. Fill out that last column.

Okay. Go down that list and, given the criteria you've just filled out, pick one of those fears. Maybe it's the one that you realized has the easiest potential "real" consequences. Maybe it's the one in Column 4 that got a 10/10. No matter what it is, pick the one that stands out to you the most, and commit to yourself that every day for the next 30 days, you will take one drastic step towards reversing that fear and achieving whatever goal you've been unwilling to go after because of it.

During the process, use what you've just learned about Motivation and Action to help push you forward.

In 30 days, come back and look at your list. Look at what you wrote down for all four columns. Have you made progress? Was it nearly as scary as you thought it was going to be? If I had to guess, you're going to be a heck of a lot further along than you imagined you could be.

Why? Because you've started retraining your brain to think towards *achieving* that goal, rather than *avoiding the pain* caused by going after it. When you tell your brain that you want to achieve something, it starts to focus differently, and the fear is no longer the focus.

Chapter 7:

The Most Important Skill You Can Learn

"Why do we fall, Bruce?
So that we can learn to pick ourselves up again."
-Batman Begins

So far, we've looked at different types of motivation and action. And later, I'm going to share with you some very powerful tools to help quell anxiety in the moment. But there's one mindset I'd like to share with you that's more powerful and important than anything else. It's the skill that helps pilots land damaged planes with dozens of lives at stake. It's what gives Navy SEALS the ability to complete their missions, even when their buddies are dead and they've sustained massive injuries.

This most important thing you can learn in your fight against fear and anxiety is **the ability to stay calm and focused and do what needs to be done.**

When it seems like the world is falling apart around you and your demons are closing in to finish the kill, your most potent weapon is to look past your fear and take immediate and uncompromising action.

I am not a Navy SEAL and have never had to land a damaged airplane. However, there was one instance in my life where I felt completely alone, literally in the dark, and the bitter sting of panic was terrifying me into paralysis.

There are times when we know we can count on other people for our own safety and well-being. But what happens when you're stranded, alone, with no phone, no idea where you are, and surrounded by complete and utter black night, forest, and highway?

I had just moved to Austin, Texas about a year earlier. I was a poor, gigging musician, taking whatever feeble-paying gigs happened to stumble my way. On this particular scorching, mid-summer Saturday, I had landed a wedding gig in Concan, TX; a place about which I knew nothing, playing with a band I had never even met before.

I packed up my drumkit into my old, black Honda Accord 2-door and, armed with only a printed map and a tank full of gas, I started the 3-hour trek to the gig. I wasn't sure what to expect on any level.

As I got further out of the city, the scene got less civilized. The road began to narrow the way country roads do. I noticed fewer buildings and more dense forest. At one point I even came to a river crossing where, after a rainy season, the swollen river was actually crossing a few inches over the road.

Against the odds, I pulled in right on time. I met the band, and for just playing together for the first time, we followed each other extraordinarily well. There's something about musicians; after awhile, you don't even have to tell each other where to go or what to do next. You start to sense it, almost like you're relying on another part of your brains to communicate with each other unconsciously. Intuition guides you.

Not knowing what circumstances were about to befall me, that type of thinking was going to be especially helpful on my way home. By the time the gig was over and I packed up the drums, it was already 11 pm and I had a full three hours alone in the car ahead of me. And I wasn't looking forward to the drive. I've had many late night drives home from gigs in other cities, and it can be tricky. Imagine going to the gym for three hours, outside in grueling heat, then fighting to stay awake with no one else around.

So, I was anxious to get back.

I said goodbye to everyone, got in the car, and drove off into the night. Now, that same road back from Concan was not some 18-lane superhighway; we're talking a dinky, two-lane, occasionally-paved road that felt more like an obstacle course.

I was about 45 minutes into the drive when I noticed a weird knocking sound coming from somewhere in my vehicle. I couldn't quite put my finger on it. I happened to be going through another small town at the time and pulled into a deserted gas station to check things out. Finding nothing under the car, I figured it was nothing and got back on the road.

About 15 miles later, I heard it again. "Tick, tick, tick, tick, tick..." Again, I let it go...because I had no choice.

I focused on the road, my two headlights the only thing lighting up the otherwise pitch black path ahead of me. My eyes started to glaze over a bit from the exhaustion. I leaned back into the seat and focused on the road.

Out of nowhere, the "check engine" light flashed on the dashboard.

A flash of panic shot down my spine. "What does that mean?" It could have been anything.

Another dashboard warning light surged to life. Then another next to it. But the car was still moving.

And there I faced a decision. I was 15 miles away from the last town, and no idea how many pitch black miles until the next one. I could try and retrace my steps, or keep lumbering on with my quickly-sinking ship and hope for the best.

I decided on the latter. My white-knuckled hands nervously glued to the wheel at 10 and 2, I stayed alert and focused as I could. After about 30 seconds, more dashboard lights came on, one after the other like horrible fireworks. My headlights started to dim, like a setting sun slowly giving way to creepy, black night. And with what little light was still remaining, I noticed a cloud of white smoke spewing out of the sides of the hood in front of me. The steering wheel became rigid, like trying to steer an oil tanker, and the gas pedal went limp.

Control, in any regard, was gone.

Not knowing if my car's engine was on fire or about to explode, I reached the point where it was obvious that I had to take action. With barely a glow left from my headlights, I found a patch of dirt on the right side, and started turning. I was able to amble the car completely off the road, stop, and get out.

With shaky hands I pulled out my phone. Nothing. Not even a roaming signal. I was in the middle of nowhere, where I doubted electricity had even been installed, let alone cell phone towers.

I was completely stranded, in darkness, with no way of contacting anyone.

With fear invading every cell in my body, I got down on my knees and leaned my head against the side of the car. I had literally reached a crossroads. I had never felt this overwhelming a sense of panic in my life. I had no idea where I was, no clue how to find my way home, and there was no one around to help. If it hadn't been for the gig money I had in my pocket, I would have barely been able to afford a box of Tic Tacs, either.

In that moment, I realized I had two choices. I could allow fear and panic to win. I could sit in the car, hope that this was a bad dream, and then somehow the car would magically fix itself and drive me back to Austin.

Or, I could accept that, these were my circumstances. And that, despite the overwhelming adrenaline and fear that were coursing through my body, I had the tools and smarts to take care of this situation and get myself home.

As the driveway ahead of me could have easily gone several miles, I knew my best bet was flagging somebody down on the highway. I opened the trunk and rifled through the maze of tightly-packed drum gear to see what I could use to get attention.

I found a pack of flares that I had stuck in there a couple years ago. The only problem, I had never lit a flare before. And with no light, I couldn't read the directions. Again, that voice of my higher self started echoing through my head: "You will figure it out."

I walked back up to the road and waited. After fumbling with the flare for several minutes in utter darkness, I got it lit. After what felt like hours, nothingness gave way to two headlines in the distance. An old pickup truck slowly made its way closer, and closer. I lifted the flare and waved my arms, not knowing exactly who or what I was signaling to help me. An old, ghostly-white pick up truck slowed and stopped, and a woman who had just gotten off work rolled down the passenger side window.

After hearing what had happened, she called the police. They got a tow-truck out there and my car and I spent the night in the next town (which, ironically, was equally as far as the last town -- I had broken down almost exactly right in the middle of the two).

That told me something. Maybe fate had decided I needed a test. There was no right answer. Looking backward to what was behind me, or looking ahead to the future; neither one would have yielded a solution. My problem was happening right there, in front of me. In complete darkness, with no obvious answers.

But once I got past not knowing how to answer the question, and getting past the fear of whether or not I could answer it, I realized that I had the solution to everything I needed, right there, in my head. No matter how drastic the circumstances; whether it was the useless phone or the sinking ship of a car or the black night or the tiny highway or the confusing flare or the smoke that clouded what little I could see; the answers were there. I just had to realize that I could find them once I had enough faith in myself to start looking.

***

Looking back on this story, it's not actually that scary. To some, it might even seem trivial. But in the moment, it was terrifying. When I look at what scared me so much, I realize that it was the fact that I had no idea what was going to happen, and so my mind was on overdrive creating images of all the horrible things that could kill me. All the "what if's" started creeping in.

"What if I can't get home?"
"What if I get robbed?"
"What if the car blows up with me in it?"
"What if I get out of the car and some animal attacks me?"

And at that moment, two things were true.

1. All of those events were absolutely possible.
2. I still had to get out of this situation and get home.

When you're in a situation where you're terrified to do something, you have a choice. You can focus on #1 -- everything that can go wrong and what terrible events can befall you.

Or, you can focus on #2. You realize that you are usually the best person to get yourself out of a bad situation. So, you rely on something called "courage" to push forward.

See, most people are misinformed on what "courage" really means. Having courage does not mean you don't feel fear. It means that you push forward and do what needs to be done *in spite* of the fear.

If you're waiting for the fear to go away to do the thing you're afraid of, you're going to be waiting a long, long time. This is because fear generally compounds on itself. The more you think about something and don't do it, the more your mind finds ways to convince you that you're going to get hurt and stay away.

Instead, you cut off your "what-if's" and just focus on what needs to be done.

I've separated this out from the "Actions" section because I believe it's not just an action...it's a mindset. It's a skill you commit yourself to practicing and developing every day, just like you would build up your muscles through daily lifting routines.

Begin to build your awareness of what you're afraid of. Sometimes, these fears are very subtle and you're so used to ignoring them, the same way you would fail to notice a beautiful flower or a homeless person as you're walking by, thinking about the various things you otherwise have going on in your life.

So cultivate that internal radar, and make a mental note when you feel a fear; especially if you avoid taking action as a result. Maybe it's something as simple as avoiding a particular checkout line at the store because you glanced at the cashier and they intimidated you. Who knows what that person is like, or what you could learn from them once you take fear into your hands and step in that line.

You tell yourself that when you experience fear, that experience is not something to avoid; it's an opportunity to help you grow. And you don't beat yourself up when you fail to seize that moment. You say, "This time, I didn't. Next time, I have to."

The more you begin to notice fears as they pop up, the more power you will have in overcoming them. You will build a default mindset of mental and emotional power, allowing you to stay calm, composed, and in control, no matter what happens. It's an incredible feeling to be able to feel capable of handling anything. And the only thing keeping you from feeling that way is practice.

TIME FOR SOME ACTION:

DEVELOPING YOUR COURAGE MINDSET

Take out another piece of paper and tack it to your wall, or put it somewhere where you'll have easy access to it. This will be your Fear Tracking Sheet.

Turn on your Fear Radar, and begin to notice whenever a particular fear comes up for you. When it does, write it down on your Tracking Sheet. When the same fear comes up again, put tick marks next to it, i.e. "Afraid to talk to my teacher about my assignment. III"

This will show you where to begin focusing your effort and energies, because you'll see what you're the most afraid of, instead of what you think you're afraid of.

Chapter 8:

The Anti-Anxiety Toolbox

"You're not going insane, Benjy."

I could hear the stress growing in my dad's voice as he did everything he could to comfort me.

"I really, really feel like it," I whimpered through heated tears. "I don't know how I'm going to get through this."

Despite the glow of soft lights and the soothing hum of the air vent above me, this tiny room had me encased me like a prison cell and I wanted out. NOW. My heavy breathing bordered on hyperventilation as I sank further down into the narrow, green vinyl chair.

The wretch of a guidance counselor next to me, in a tone that landed somewhere between feigned empathy and utter boredom, cackled, "Maybe try counting down from 100 again?"

Yeah, right. I'm sure that'll work this time, despite its utter uselessness the last three times she suggested it.

"Dad, I don't know what to do," I said, ignoring her. "I can't handle this. I don't think I'll ever be able to go back down there."

"Well, I think you're going to have to try," he pleaded. "You can't stay stuck in there forever."

And he was right.

***

No matter what our fears, it's very difficult to live a rich, meaningful life while hiding behind what scares us.

That day was one of the last times I experienced a full-blown panic attack. I had just started junior high school, and it was hitting me hard. Each time, I would be sitting in Mrs. Rich's science class, and this inexplicable sense of fear and impending danger would quickly escalate from a bubble of uneasiness into emotional torment like hearing a blaring fire alarm combined with getting eaten alive.

The same scene had now happened several times over the last few weeks, and with each one, I would slink quickly out of class and, not knowing where else to go, I would hurry up to the guidance counselor's office. They would allow me to sit in a room by myself and call my dad in a desperate attempt to make it go away. The calls would calm me enough to become functional again, but quite simply, they were a band-aid that kept falling off a wound that needed a much stronger anesthetic.

And so my parents took me to begin working, for the first time, with a therapist. I didn't know what to expect; it felt like there was no way this was going to get fixed. But I gave it a shot.

I still remember walking into Dr. Steve's office for the first time. He was welcoming, warm, and understanding, helping me explore and eventually unearth where these anxieties were rooted and what was likely causing the attacks.

But that is not a speedy (nor easy) process. We had several months of work ahead of us. But before that happened, he knew he had to get me to stay in class. To do that, we were going to have to focus directly on the attacks themselves. So he set out to teach me coping strategies that would allow me to calm myself down as soon as I felt a panic attack coming on.

He told me, "These are very easy to perform, and you can do most of them without anyone even noticing."

What follows are Dr. Steve's exercises for calming yourself down when you start to feel anxiety. They got me through the rest of 7th grade, a bar mitzvah, several college exams and job interviews. And a couple really bad first dates.

Anti-Anxiety Training

Before we get into these, I want you to note what I said above. These exercises are not designed to end your anxiety once and for all. Any book that claims it can do so fails to take into account the fact that we are all different and require solid work and focus to address our individual problems. I am a strong believer in working with a therapist to help overcome your major fears and hang-ups, as only then can someone custom tailor an answer for your custom-made problems.

Instead, these are here to give you temporary relief when you are in the moment and your fear is paralyzing you from taking action or being able to function.

By the way, talking to a therapist does *not* mean you're crazy. It's like going to an impartial friend or teacher to help you work through a problem. Think of them the same way you would hire a math tutor to help you get through Calculus...only much more rewarding and with fewer calculators. (And for the record, I'd much rather go to therapy than attempt Calculus.)

Exercise #1: Belly Breathing
I've mentioned elsewhere in the book that taking long, deliberate breaths is a signal to your body that all is calm and we can stop worrying. Normal deep breaths are better than short breaths. However, breathing from your stomach is far more powerful and effective.

Try this: Place your dominant hand (the one you use to write with) over your stomach. Over the course of five whole seconds, breathe in so that your hand gets pushed out while you're doing it. Hold that breath for a full second. Then, exhale for another five whole seconds. Wait one full second. Then repeat the whole sequence: five in, hold one, five out, wait one. Do so for a good 5 to 10 minutes.

If you're having trouble making this work, you can just take regular deep breaths, and just focus on breathing from your gut. If you're having trouble making your stomach rise and actually breathing from that area, try laying down on a solid surface, preferably like the floor or a mat.

When you first attempt this exercise, it may seem a little tough. If you're used to breathing a certain way, attempting to do so differently is going to seem weird. But with a little practice, you'll get it in no time.

Exercise #2: Squeezing the Grape

This one requires a little mind work, but it's easy and virtually imperceptible. I used to practice this out in the schoolyard, and nobody noticed.

Open one of your hands fully, and then with your other hand, pretend to put one big, juicy grape in your palm and close your fingers around it so you can imagine yourself holding it firmly, but not crushing it.

Give yourself a count of three, and then suddenly, squeeze your hand so hard that you can feel that grape popping and bursting in your hand. Keep squeezing, harder and harder, feeling the tension in your fingers, hand, wrist, and arm growing tighter and tighter with every passing moment. Even when you feel like you can't squeeze any harder, lock down even more. Squeeze all the juice out of that imaginary grape. Tighter, tighter, harder, harder....and stop.

Drop the "grape" and notice the feeling of relaxation flowing through your fingers, your hand, your wrist, up your lower arm, through your elbow, up through your bicep and tricep, into your shoulder, and then into your entire body. You feel more and more relaxed, knowing you've rid yourself of any tension and anxiety.

Try this, and if it works for you a little the first time, don't be afraid to try it once or twice more.

Exercise #3: Tensing/Untensing Your Jaw

This is similar to the Grape Squeezing exercise, except you're using your jaw muscles, which can carry an inordinate amount of tension.

Begin by opening your mouth and trying to relax your jaw as much as you can. Let it hang there for a moment, and then calmly close your mouth and jaw. Focus on where your upper and lower jaws meet at your back teeth, just for a few moments.

Give yourself another count of three, and with your already-closed jaw, clench them together as hard as you can and hold them there. Push harder and harder, until you can barely stand it. Then, push even harder. Hold it...hold it...and, release.

Again, feel the tension seep out of your jaw, your mouth, your entire head and neck, feel the relaxation flow down your spine into your lower back and radiating into your arms and legs, almost like soothing sunshine warming your skin. Imagine yourself as a ball of soothing white light, in harmony with everything around you. Fear does not exist. Worry is over. The only thing is love, connection, and peace.

Ahhh.

Okay, note on this one too. If you have a sensitive jaw or begin feeling pain while doing this exercise, STOP. You're better off to use the other exercises. Plus, my attorney said I should mention that I'm not liable for any dental work that arises from your implementation of using this one.

Exercise #4: Core Power

By now you're probably getting the idea of how these "progressive relaxation" techniques work. I have one more of the same style for you.

Instead of your fist or your jaw, you're going to feel this one in your stomach. Your core is also one of the strongest and most influential groups of muscles in your body, so let's give them a workout to help them, and you, relax.

It helps if you're sitting down for this one, but you can do it standing up as well. If you have to stand, it's a little easier if you lean over about 30 degrees.

Run your hand over your stomach and abs for a moment. By doing this, you're establishing a mental connection with that part of your body to increase awareness of it. This will help you stay more present, which will pull attention away from your fears and anxieties.

When you're ready, clench your ab and stomach muscles as hard as you can. Continue to breathe normally while keeping that area tighter and tighter. Hold that clench and focus on the tension and tightness. Be aware of all your energy flowing to that spot while you maintain normal breaths. Hold it...hold it...at least another 10 seconds...5 seconds...and, relax.

More relaxation and soothing calm spreading all around your body.

Repeat.

Exercise #5: Beach Visualization

The only muscle you're going to use during this exercise is your brain. Visualization is a very powerful technique; one used by actors, artists, athletes, and other top performers to put them in a more focused state.

You can use visualization to make yourself a peak performer, and you can also use it to take yourself to the peak of relaxation.

Begin by finding a nice, quiet place where you won't be disturbed for about 20 minutes. You can cut this down to as few as 5 minutes if necessary, but the longer you indulge in the activity, the more benefits you'll feel.

If you like, put on a pair of headphones and find a track, whether through iTunes, YouTube, or otherwise (I love the free ones on YouTube) of soothing beach sounds, like waves, birds, etc. Make sure the track lasts for the amount of time you intend on doing the exercise. I sometimes even use the end of the track as my unofficial timer so I know when to stop.

Get comfortable, and when you're ready, close your eyes.

Begin by imagining yourself on the most beautiful beach in the world. The sand is white and glassy, the water is clear and shimmering, and the sun is warming the air around you to the perfect temperature. You begin walking down the beach and feel the sand in between your toes and you sink a bit and settle in. It surrounds your feet, warming your soles and toes. You look to your right, and the expanse of the ocean stretches on for miles and miles, as far as you can see.

On your left is a forest, green, lush, and beautiful, and you slowly notice little hints of color dabbing through the green. You realize these bits of color are actually stunning, vibrant tropical birds, and as you walk by, they hop to attention and are happy you've arrived. Each one flaps its wings in excitement a couple times and lets out a little, gleeful chirp. It brings a smile to your face as you keep walking.

You notice a reflection coming from the sand ahead of you. As you get close, you find a nice pool of water, clean, clear and safe. You dip a toe into the water and feel it envelop your skin. It's so soothing that you decide to slowly enter the pool, and it's just deep enough that you can fit your entire body in, reclining on the bottom, with your head comfortably above water.

You continue laying there for as long as you like. With each passing moment, any tension in your body evaporates into the air and away so that you never see it again. You feel relaxation like never before. It lasts and lasts, and feels wonderful.

You decide it's time to leave the pool and come back to the present moment. Begin counting down from 10, slowly. With each number you become more aware of your surroundings, where your hands, feet, and other parts of your body are. As you get closer to 1, you feel present and focused. You're awake and aware and ready to take on the day.

When you reach 1, open your eyes. Take in what's going on around you, always remembering that you can return to this paradise any time you wish.

Chapter 9:
Conclusion

"The only thing we have to fear, is fear itself."
-Franklin D. Roosevelt

Yeah right, FDR. It wasn't "fear" I was afraid of the first time I watched *Jaws*. I was afraid of 25-foot monster Great White Sharks that were going to break into my house through the sewer line and pull me into the ocean, just like they did Captain Quint.

We have incredibly powerful minds and highly evolved bodies. After millions of years of developing the most advanced and powerful ways to stay alive, our internal alert sirens have a way of making certain things completely and utterly terrifying, even if they shouldn't be.

Our fears feel very, very real. And when we're afraid, we tend not to act.

But what would your life be like if those fears were stripped away? What if, even when you felt the butterflies come up, you took action and just did it?

How would life be different?

What could you achieve?

How would it change how you see the world, or even how you see yourself?

Whether it's how you do your job, going after a new career, starting your own business, pursuing the guy or girl, or even taming a shark, fears keep us all from doing certain things in our lives. So what's stopping you from being the kind of person who doesn't let fear get in the way of what you want for yourself?

And after you answer that question, answer this one:

Do I deserve to live without fear and go after (and even get) everything I could ever want?

If you answered yes, then remind yourself every single day that this is the life you deserve. Stop at nothing to achieve it.

If you answered no, then you ought to do some serious thinking. Because if you don't believe that you deserve to be happy, that's where you start. Maybe someone told you at some point in your life that you aren't worthy of happiness. Or aren't capable of it.

Bullsh*t.

You ARE worthy and capable of being happy. How do I know that? Because there's nothing you can tell me that would change my mind. We've all done things we regret in life. We've all taken shortcuts, hurt people, or acted in ways we later wish we hadn't.

But it's never too late to change course. Take bold and decisive action today – right now – to become the person you've always dreamed of being. Even if you miss the mark, you'll still have made the effort.

And when you get to the point in your life when you look back and ask yourself, "Did I do everything I could to live my life boldly and proudly?", you can raise your fists to the heavens and scream, "YES! I DID!"

I'd like to leave you with a quote from from Jim Carrey's Commencement Address at the 2014 Maharishi University of Management (available on YouTube, if you're interested).

"So many of us choose our path out of fear, disguised as practicality. What we really want seems impossibly out of reach and ridiculous to expect, so we never dare to ask the universe for it...My father could have been a great

comedian, but he didn't believe that was possible for him. So he made a conservative choice. Instead, he got a 'safe' job as an accountant. And when I was 12 years old, he was let go from that 'safe' job and our family had to do whatever we could to survive. I learned many great lessons from my father, not the least of which was that you can fail at what you DON'T want, so you might as well take a chance on doing what you love."

Thank you for including me and this book on your path to becoming louder and stronger. I hope to meet you one day, hear the story of your own struggle, and learn from you as well.

Be well. Be bold. Adventure greatly.

You already have everything you need. Now, get to it.

BONUS!

Thank you for investing your time, effort, and hard-earned bucks to check out **TAMING A SHARK**.

However, this was just the beginning. I want to help and support you as much as I can, and so I'm offering an ***additional, super-secret chapter AND set of mini-missions*** for you to put into action and go even further on your fear-conquering journey.

To access the chapter and mini-missions, go to **www.TamingAShark.com/free-chap**

All you have to do is enter your email address, and the goods are yours.

I have additional resources, audio programs, coaching programs, and lots of free goodies on my website, **www.BenjaminPortnoy.com**

Thanks again, and see you soon.

BENJY PORTNOY

Made in the USA
Lexington, KY
05 August 2015